hc

D0236074

Feelings

Lonely

Sarah Medina

Illustrated by Jo Brooker

www.raintreepublishers.co.uk
Visit our website to find out more information about **Raintree** books.

To order:
☎ Phone 44 (0) 1865 888112
▤ Send a fax to 44 (0) 1865 314091
▢ Visit the Raintree Bookshop at **www.raintreepublishers.co.uk** to browse our catalogue and order online.

First published in Great Britain by Raintree,
Halley Court, Jordan Hill, Oxford OX2 8EJ,
part of Harcourt Education.
Raintree is a registered trademark of
Harcourt Education Ltd.

© Harcourt Education Ltd 2008
The moral right of the proprietor has
been asserted.

Editorial: Diyan Leake and Cassie Mayer
Design: Joanna Hinton-Malivoire
Picture research: Erica Martin
Illustration: Jo Brooker
Production: Duncan Gilbert

Originated by Dot Gradations
Printed and bound in China by
  South China Printing Company

ISBN 978 1 4062 0777 4
12 11 10 09 08
10 9 8 7 6 5 4 3 2 1

British Library Cataloguing in Publication Data
Medina, Sarah
  Lonely. - (Feelings)
  1. Loneliness - Juvenile literature
  I. Title
  155.9'2

Acknowledgements
The publishers would like to thank the following
for permission to reproduce photographs:
Bananastock p. **22A, B, D**; Getty Images pp. **6**
(Photodisc), **22C** (Taxi).

Every effort has been made to contact copyright
holders of any material reproduced in this book.
Any omissions will be rectified in subsequent
printings if notice is given to the publishers.

Contents

Some words are shown in bold, **like this**. They are explained in the glossary on page 23.

What is loneliness?

Loneliness is a **feeling**. Feelings are something you feel inside. Everyone has different feelings all the time.

worried

happy

sad

When you are lonely, you feel all on your own. You may feel that no one likes you or wants to play with you.

What happens when I am lonely?

When you are lonely, you might feel very sad. You might feel like crying sometimes.

You may feel **bored** and want someone to play with. Sometimes, you might feel angry and unhappy.

Why do I get lonely?

You may feel lonely if your family moves house. It might take some time before you make new friends.

Being left out of games can make you feel lonely. If your friends are on holiday, you may miss them.

Is it OK to feel lonely?

It is normal to feel lonely from time to time. The important thing is what you do when you feel lonely.

It is not good to feel lonely for too long. Do everything you can to help your loneliness pass.

What can I do when I feel lonely?

If you are lonely, tell an adult. Perhaps they can take you somewhere to make new friends.

Try starting a new **hobby**, and share something you have made with your classmates. You can also do something kind for someone else.

Will I always feel lonely?

It is normal for **feelings** to change over time. You will not feel lonely for ever. Soon you will feel better.

14

Remember to ask for help and to do things that you enjoy. Then your loneliness will pass more quickly.

How can I tell if someone is lonely?

When people are lonely, they may sit by themselves. They may look sad or upset.

They might look as if they do not care.
But often they just think that no one
will want to play with them.

Can I help when someone is lonely?

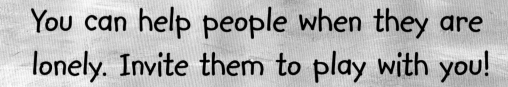

You can help people when they are lonely. Invite them to play with you!

If you see someone who looks lonely at school, ask that person to sit with you.

Am I the only one who feels lonely?

Remember, everyone feels lonely sometimes. You will not always feel lonely!

It is good to learn what to do about loneliness. Then you can help yourself and help other people, too.

What are these feelings?

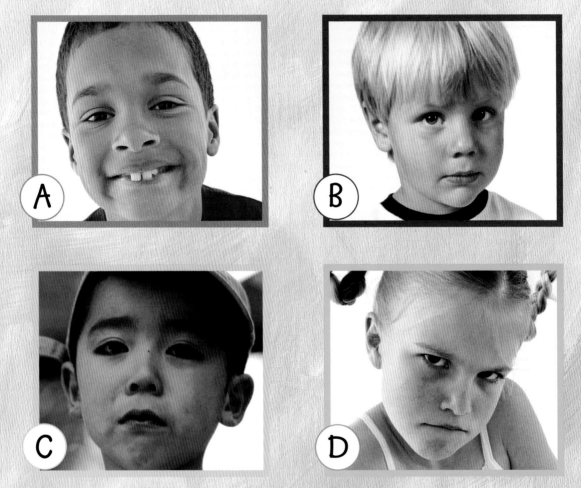

A

B

C

D

Which of these people looks happy?
What are the other people feeling?
Look at page 24 to see the answers.

Picture glossary

bored
when you are not interested in what you are doing

feeling
something that you feel inside. Loneliness is a feeling.

hobby
something you like doing for fun

Index

Answers to the questions on page 22

The person in picture A looks happy. The other people could be lonely, angry, or sad.

Note to Parents and Teachers

Reading for information is an important part of a child's literacy development. Learning begins with a question about something. Help children think of themselves as investigators and researchers by encouraging their questions about the world around them. Most chapters in this book begin with a question. Read the question together. Look at the pictures. Talk about what you think the answer might be. Then read the text to find out if your predictions were correct. Think of other questions you could ask about the topic, and discuss where you might find the answers. Assist children in using the picture glossary and the index to practice new vocabulary and research skills.